The Railways of

NORTH-WEST ENGLAND

in the Latter Days of Steam

Malcolm Castledine

ISBN 1 901945 39 1

DEDICATION

To the memory of my one time boss and friend, the late William (Bill) Pemberton, whose main passion was music. However, as Bill's Dad had been an engine driver at Saltley, I'm sure he had a latent passion for steam locomotives (Black 5's in particular), and on occasions he would join us at the lineside just to take in the atmosphere of a passing steam hauled special train.

First published in the United Kingdom
by Book Law Publications 2005
382 Carlton Hill, Nottingham, NG4 1JA
Printed and bound by The Amadeus Press, Cleckheaton, West Yorkshire

INTRODUCTION

My introduction to the railways of north-west England took place in November 1962 which, with hindsight, was not a good time because most steam locomotive classes had already seen withdrawals reducing their number, some on a catastrophic scale which was to render them extinct. However, 1962 was not a bad time either because I managed to see, just, some of the threatened locomotive types before they disappeared. So, in retrospect, you could say I got there just in time and hopefully my camera has preserved those images from that era which still means so much to many of us that experienced it.

What I did not realise in 1962, nor did many other people I suspect, was the fact that north-west England was going to become the last bastion of British Railways steam power. The other fact was that only six years remained in which to record the working steam locomotive. We had a few harsh winters to contend with before the end came so the opportunity for railway photography was taken basically when the weather was decent or if one visited a different location to one's usual patch of ground. Basically there did not seem to be any hurry as the change over was going to take many more years yet; we had been led to believe at some time in the 1970's.

I suppose the panic set in for most enthusiasts about 1967 when the Southern and then the North Eastern Region gave up their last remnants of steam power. I personally responded by taking a quick one day trip to the Southern in March. Then off to the North-East for ten days or so in July. A trip over to Carlisle on the intervening Saturday was rewarded with what was possibly the last phase of regular steam hauled passenger trains. But in 1962 nothing of what was to come even entered our minds and we just got on with what was available during the sometimes painful transition.

Crewe locomotive works had always held a fascination for me and my first visit was quite eye-opening. Firstly there was the scale of the place to contend with and then the diversity of the locomotive types. I managed to take numerous photographs but never enough because there was not enough time, I did not have copious rolls of film at my disposal and light was a little bit scarce at that time of year. If I had been left to my own devices, with time and film, I could easily have spent all the hours of daylight at the works probably recording every single locomotive of the one hundred plus residents on that day. Later, in 1963, I was a member of the East Midlands RCTS party which had been brought into the works by train and Crewe was just part of the itinerary - next stop Horwich works!

After the 1963 RCTS trip I started to venture over to Crewe and beyond under my own steam and Chester, Buxton, Manchester and Preston were all visited at some time. Then I went further northwards and eventually got to Carlisle via Newcastle. Of course the engine sheds at Rose Grove, Lostock Hall and Carnforth beckoned but they did not get my attention until 1968 and in the meantime I wanted to get as much main line action as I could. Oxenholme and Tebay seemed like good places to be in 1964 and 1965, and only every other train was diesel hauled but the surviving Stanier Pacifics, once the pride of the line, were by now relegated to freight working, although some sleeper trains still had them as power during that last year but night photography was still not a viable proposition - it was difficult enough to see the 'Duchess' passing through Oxenholme station at 60 m.p.h. at one a.m., let alone photograph it.

The summer months of 1968 will go down in history as the last days of BR steam and so it was for us enthusiasts and photographers who spent most weekends visiting the Lancashire engine sheds just before they closed. Closures became a way of life and film was being exposed at a tremendous rate with most surviving locomotives becoming legends overnight simply because of the amount of photographs taken of each one. Then, suddenly it was all gone. No more BR steam - forever.

Thankfully I had my photographic record, much of it still in negative form until last year, and I was invited by my publisher to put this album of north-west railways and steam locomotives together. Hopefully you too will derive as much pleasure from it as I have in putting it together.

Malcolm Castledine, Long Eaton, 2005.

47389

(opposite) The former London & North Western engine shed at Chester became the last bastion of steam in the city and was operational until 5th June 1967. On Sunday 27th March 1966 the depot offered a mixture of locomotives with Stanier Class 5's being in abundance. Amongst the 'rarer items' was this forty year old 'Jinty', No.47389, looking the worse for wear but nevertheless still in employment. It was withdrawn in July and ended up in Liverpool being scrapped there by Messrs. Maden & McKee at the end of the year. Considering its birthplace was at Vulcan Foundry, from were it emerged in 1926 as LMS No.16472, and that most of its working life was spent around the Mersey basin at ex LNWR sheds such as Plodder Lane, Birkenhead and latterly Chester, it was perhaps appropriate that its demise should take place in the same area. Immediately behind the 0-6-0T is former Great Western 0-6-2T No.6697, a Collett 1924 design which was hanging on to life and was amongst the last of the operational GWR engines. Having started life coal hauling in the Welsh valleys, it got to the Northwest from Barry shed via Leamington. At the rear of the line is BR Standard Class 5 No.73160, one of the few of its class to work in the Newcastle area when new but it soon moved from Blaydon down to more familiar territory at Normanton in September 1957. After nearly nine years in Yorkshire it went south to Bletchley in April 1964 then to Oxley in the following January. Within four months it was sent to join its numerous sister engines based at Patricroft shed and from there worked out its final years being withdrawn in November 1967. It would have worked into Chester from Manchester on either a stopping passenger or parcels train. Its last journey, in March 1968, took it from Patricroft to Great Bridge in the West Midlands where Cashmore's cut it up alongside many other steam locomotives. On the opposite side of the coal stage are a couple of Stanier Cl.5's which were stored pending withdrawal.

Seeing as this Collett 0-6-2T is the only GWR engine featured in this album, I feel it is worthwhile to include a fuller picture of its 68-ton bulk. It was, at the time of this photograph in March 1966, allocated to Birkenhead shed as Chester 6A had no ex GWR engines on its books at that time. Of course, up to April 1960 the engines with copper capped chimneys had their own residence at Chester situated in the triangle of lines just north of Chester (General) station, but in that year they were evicted to make way for diesel multiple units, although since 1957 the steam allocation had been slowly diminishing. The GWR had been associated with the city since the 1850's when the Chester & Birkenhead Railway had opened a shed, and then in 1870 the GWR took over the older (1840) and adjacent Chester & Crewe Railway engine shed from the L&NWR when that company moved to its new and larger eight road premises to the east of the city. Up to World War Two, Chester based GWR engines worked daily to Manchester (Exchange) and were serviced at Patricroft shed before returning home but, after the end of hostilities those particular working were not resumed and apparently no other GW locomotives ever visited 'Cottonopolis' again. The GWR link between Chester and Manchester was probably at its strongest prior to 1900 when at least a half dozen goods and passenger engines were sub-shedded from Chester to Ordsall Lane shed then later, when that shed was closed, to Patricroft depot. Again war changed much of the traffic patterns and daily visits from Chester based engines to Manchester had to suffice. But that was all a long time ago (as is 1966 now - isn't that the year we won some trophy after beating an old arch enemy again).

My first visit to Crewe was on 11th November 1962 when I went to North shed, South shed and the locomotive works. The end of 1962 was indeed a period of transition with many of the famous Stanier Pacific's working out the last years of their lives or, as was the case with some members of the 'Princess Royal' class, were now condemned and were being cut up. Such was the case with No.46209 PRINCESS BEATRICE seen here in the works Stripping shop on Sunday 11th November 1962, minus tender but still intact. Barely twenty-seven years old, this majestic lady was reduced to small pieces of scrap metal the very next day. It took weeks to put these engines together when being built, heavy general repairs could take anything from three to nine weeks to complete yet the scrapmen could take them apart in a matter of hours. Withdrawn at the end of the previous September, 46209 had completed over one and a half million revenue earning miles transiting the West Coast Main Line during its life, with 1936 being its busiest year when it ran over a hundred thousand miles even though it spent nearly five weeks in works under repair. Unlike most of the class, it was never allocated to Polmadie or any Scottish depot, its furthest northern outpost being Upperby where it stayed for only a few weeks in August 1960. It had spent much of 1961 in store at Crewe North shed clocking up just over 14,000 revenue miles that year and after moving to Camden at the end of January 1962 it again languished at that shed although it did double its annual mileage on the previous twelve months. Going into store at the end of the Summer timetable period, it never worked again and was condemned on the 24th September.

Staying in the Stripping shop during that November 1962 visit, I photographed 'Patriot' No.45538 GIGGLESWICK with its nameplates still in place going through the throes of scrapping. The smokebox door is unceremoniously dumped on the floor from where it fell after the hinges had been cut away during the previous morning, probably the last action taken on the engine before the workmen clocked off on Saturday lunchtime. 1962 had been a bad year for the 'Patriot' class with no less than twenty-five of them being withdrawn that year, including the last of the thirty-four unrebuilt examples. No.45538 had been condemned in September. Crewe works dealt with most of this mass 1962 condemnation, with Horwich works helping out with a couple such as 45507 and 45518. By 1965 the 'Patriot' class was history but compared with other classes of LMS express passenger locomotives they had virtually managed to fulfil their 30-year 'intended' operational lifetime. Forty of the class had been built at Crewe between 1932 and 1934 with the other dozen built by Derby, two in 1930 and ten in 1933.

46208

(opposite) Flanked by former LNWR Super D tenders, 'Princess Royal' No.46208 PRINCESS HELENA VICTORIA awaits its turn to enter the stripping shop where in just a few days it will cease to exist. Luckily the nameplates and numberplate were saved from the melting pot and are still with us today. Ironically any one of those nameplates could command a sum far greater than the cost of the locomotive and its tender when it was built in 1935. This was another of the class which worked only from English sheds, its last being Edge Hill where it had been allocated for the previous eleven years. Note that the shed has removed the 8A shedplate before consigning the engine to its last journey. No doubt some Type 4 diesel locomotive would benefit from its fitting. Except for the two preserved engines, 46201 and 46203, and the class leader 46200 PRINCESS ROYAL which was scrapped at J&N. Connell in Coatbridge in November 1964, this was the last of the class dealt with at Crewe works. Regarding mileage's, again, 1936 had seen this particular engine's best performances and the last two years its worst with a total of just over 34,000 in that period - no doubt the arrival of the English Electric Type 4 diesels had something to do with its irregular appearances on the *MERSEYSIDE EXPRESS.* So, we bid farewell to a class which although sharing the same traffic as the 'Duchesses', never seemed to get the same amount of adulation or limelight as their streamlined brethren.

To end the November 1962 visit to Crewe works, we finish on a more positive note with this illustration of Ivatt Cl.2 2-6-0 No.46504 which had just completed a Heavy General overhaul. The works was still carrying out all manner of overhauls and repair to steam locomotives during 1962 and would continue to do so for a number of years to come (see later). The Oswestry based mogul was the second engine of the Swindon built batch (46503 - 46527), all of which came into traffic during 1952 and 1953. All were allocated to the Western Region, note the GWR type lamp brackets, and had minor repairs carried out at Oswestry works whilst major repairs took place at Swindon. The latter works continued to paint these engines in fully lined green livery and when Crewe took over the major overhauls of the WR based Class 2's, they too carried on the Swindon paint tradition, at least for a couple of years. Although forty-two of the once 128 strong class lasted until 1967, the fourteen year old No.46504 was withdrawn in October 1966 and followed many of its kin to Cashmore's Great Bridge yard for scrapping. Note the Stanier Cl.5 behind, No.45436, is also fully lined at this time but with a proper Crewe finish in black.

Crewe North shed on 11th November 1962 had a profusion of ex LMS types side by side with various diesel locomotives. However, steam was still holding its own although this view of 'Jubilee' No.45552 SILVER JUBILEE suggests otherwise but it was November and many locomotives were in a state of winter storage from which many would never come back to life whilst others were revived to spend another year on the main line. No.45552, or should it be No.45642 ?, was intact and complete with nameplates, smokebox number plate and its unique cabside mounted raised numbers (which were in fact wooden cut-outs by now as was, apparently, one of the nameplates). It 'officially' had nearly two years of life left before its September 1964 withdrawal but I never did see it working again so I cannot vouch as to its activity or otherwise. This locomotive started life at Crewe works in November 1934 as No.5642 and in the following year it changed identities with No.5552, another Crewe product from May 1934 and the actual first member of the class. As the new class leader in 1935, No.5552 picked up the SILVER JUBILEE title whilst the 'new' 5642 became BOSCAWEN in 1936. Moves were afoot in the latter days of steam to have this engine preserved but alas nothing came of it and it was sold to Cashmore's at Great Bridge in December 1964 and went the way of thousands of other steam locomotives in that decade. The engine had been on the Crewe North books since June 1961 when it had vacated Edge Hill shed after a five year residency there.

It was always nice to see Stanier's superb 'Duchess' class either at work or resting and what better place to see them doing the latter than Crewe North shed. In November 1962 all thirty-eight of the class were still active and Crewe North had plenty on offer for my visit. Being a Nottingham lad, born and bred, I had a soft spot for No.46251 CITY OF NOTTINGHAM and though I did not know it at the time, I was to have the privilege of seeing and photographing this magnificent engine in my home town and at my favourite engine shed, Annesley, when it came to work a Railway Correspondence & Travel Society special in 1964. On this day it wasn't quite as clean as it was to be for the special working but nevertheless it was in a presentable condition, as were most of the Crewe North's allocation of engines at that time, and it was still used for hauling the West Coast Main Line's premier expresses.

Another resident 'Duchess' was No.46248 CITY OF LEEDS, which was wonderfully clean and a tribute to the die-hard shed staff at Crewe who were still trying their best to maintain a dignified appearance their engines deserved. 46248 had just been got ready for a one month storage and it was to be 8th December before it was back out on the main line. Except for just over five years spent at Camden over various periods of time, and four months at Upperby on two separate occasions, this engine had spent the rest of its life working from Crewe North. Its demise came on 5th September 1964, a bad year for the class which ceased to exist by the end of the following month. In November 1964 it joined a procession which took the remaining Pacifics on a one-way trip to the West Midlands, purchased for scrap with eight others of its ilk by Cashmore's Great Bridge yard.

(right) No.46226 was visiting 5A on that second Sunday of November 1962. Upperby based DUCHESS OF NORFOLK had been Carlisle since October 1956 after a somewhat interesting eighteen years moving from different sheds which included the three usual English WCML sheds but not Polmadie, however, it was allocated to a Welsh shed and also to two different Liverpool depots. When new in May 1938, as one of the twenty-four streamlined examples of the class, it went to Camden shed to work the Glasgow services but just after the outbreak of WW2 it was sent to Speke Junction shed on 16th September 1939 for indefinite storage which in the event only lasted until 2nd October when it was sent to Holyhead. Two months later it returned to Camden and five months after that to Crewe North for a three year spell. In May 1943 it went south again to Camden and having survived the war moved to Upperby in October 1946. In 1948, whilst still a Carlisle engine, its streamlined casing was removed. June 1951 saw it back at Camden for three months before it returned to Upperby. Two years later it went to Edge Hill in November 1953 as a stand-in for one of the 'Princess Royals' undergoing overhaul, after which it went north again to Carlisle. Edge Hill got it once again during January, February and March 1955 after which it returned to Upperby. In September 1956 Crewe North shed had the 'Duchess' once more for a few weeks before it went back to Upperby. for the next eight years it plied the WCML between London and Glasgow but by the summer of 1964 its services were no longer required and withdrawal beckoned. That came on the 12th September and by January 1965 the Pacific had made its final journey, along with the other Upperby Stanier Pacifics:- 46225, 46237, 46238, 46244, 46250, 46255 and 46257, to the West of Scotland Shipbreaking Co. yard at Troon.

(overleaf) When the LMS had ceased to exist and British Railways had come into being, the future of the Stanier Pacifics looked far rosier than what actually happened. Most of them, in 1948, were barely ten years old and many much younger with the latest one, 46257 just coming into traffic. Considering that BR looked upon these engines as having a book life of at least thirty years then some or even all the class of 'Duchesses' should run into the 1970's and perhaps beyond. On that line of reasoning it was decided to completely update the facilities at Crewe North motive power depot and to create a super depot for steam locomotives, after all the shed building were nearly all ancient and worn out with the oldest, in 1948, some eighty-three years old. The grand plan included two new circular roundhouses, each with a 70ft articulated turntable, two coaling plants and four ash plants, all to be built on the site of the two running sheds and the adjacent Stock shed which was now redundant. Demolition of the latter took effect in 1950 so that erection of the first roundhouse could begin. Simultaneously mechanical coaling and ash disposal plants were erected in specific areas of the yard and by 1953 the scheme was beginning to take shape. The mechanical servicing facilities were virtually complete and a twelve road portion of the first of the roundhouses was being used. Then, the Modernisation Plan was envisaged, and eventually published, resulting in work on the Crewe North site being halted. Diesel traction would replace steam locomotives and by 1970 all BR steam would be banished - what chance the completion of the grand scheme for 5A - Nil! In this picture of 46228 DUCHESS OF RUTLAND, we can see above the engine's boiler three of the towers of the coal and ash plants which at least for ten years served the depot when it most needed such appliances. This is another of the 'Duchesses' with an interesting allocation history. New in June 1938, it went to Camden shed to work the WCML expresses but when war was declared it was sent for storage to Longsight, where, or so the authorities believed, it would be out of range of German bombers. With room at 9A something of a premium, the engine stayed only from 15th to 21st September 1939, after which it moved down to Rugby shed where it was stored from 27th September to 2nd October and then it moved again, following 6226 to Holyhead. By April 1940, when it was realised it would be more useful to have such a powerful locomotive where it was most needed, it was back at Crewe North shed. Again it followed 6226 to Camden in May 1943 and then to Upperby in October 1946. Losing its streamlined casing in 1947, it once again followed sister engine 46226 to Camden in the summer of 1951 and trailed home to Upperby after the end of the summer timetable. There was obviously some memorandum somewhere within the BR motive power offices which ordered Upperby to supply a Pacific to Edge Hill shed whenever required, and so in June 1954 and again during the following September 46228 found employment on the MERSEYSIDE EXPRESS, amongst other heavy jobs required by 8A. Crewe North got it for two year from September 1957 and finally it came back to 5A to stay in the early 1960's. During the last four months of 1963 it was stored n a serviceable condition and went back into traffic before Christmas of that year. The end came on 12th September 1964 with Cashmore's at Great Bridge having the benefit of its 160 tons of scrap metal.

46228
DUCHESS OF RUTLAND
48

This is No.46253 CITY OF ST ALBANS stored, yes it really is, inside the built portion of the new No.1 roundhouse in November 1962. Put into serviceable storage on 3rd October before my visit, it remained in that condition until 29th November when it was declared 'Unserviceable' and continued stored until 26th January 1963 when it was condemned. Disposal was rapid enough - it was taken into the nearby works and never seen again. It was probably one of the cleanest locomotives cut up during that period of crazy transition. One wonders just what catastrophe had overtaken it to declare it as being unfit - perhaps the cold winter of 1962-63 had something to do with it. If any reader knows the specific reason for its demise, I would be pleased to hear from them via the publisher. Just look at what bright and airy places the new roundhouses would have been - ideal for photography ? probably.

To round off the November 1962 trip to Crewe I next went to South shed, not the most glamorous compared with North but still an interesting place where, on Sunday visit, one could catch up to half a dozen ex Great Western engines of the 'Hall' and 'Grange' classes. Besides, over on the other side of the Shrewsbury line was Gresty Lane engine shed where again six or more copper-capped engines of all denominations could be found simmering away with not a soul in sight. However, the position and somewhat cramped space of the two road GWR shed made it difficult to photograph so I did not bother in November 1962 especially when daylight was the shortest period of the day. On South shed this Stanier mogul, No.42952, looks about ready for the scrap yard but it still had lots of life left, and it would be September 1964 before it was condemned and a further year before Central Wagon Co. at Wigan got to grips with it. Alongside is another of the 2-6-0s allocated to 5B, No.42980. Though in just the same external condition as 42952, it was to have an even longer existence and was active until late 1965, condemned in January 1966 and cut up at T.W.Ward's yard at Killamarsh during the spring. Shortly after my visit the two moguls were transferred to Stoke shed along with six others from the Crewe South stud, Nos.42948, 42949, 42959, 42961, 42963 and 42972.

Another Upperby visitor to Crewe that Sunday in November 1962 was one of the Derby built 'Royal Scots' No.46157 THE ROYAL ARTILLERYMAN. It had probably brought in a fitted freight or parcels train from Carlisle as the passenger train engines tended still to go to North shed for servicing. Since 1930, when it emerged from Derby works, this engine had had no less than thirty transfers to sheds in England, Scotland and Wales. It had worked mainly on the WCML but during the late 1950's it had worked on the old Midland Division a couple of times, firstly at Kentish Town shed from October 1957 to June 1958 when it returned to Camden. Then, in November 1959 it moved to Nottingham for eighteen months working the expresses to St Pancras before moving over to Saltley in June 1961 for a one year stint. In June 1962 it went to Carlisle Upperby and then in the following June to Kingmoor to face withdrawal in January 1964, a year in which twenty-one other 'Scots' got the chop leaving only five operational members of the class which all succumbed in 1965. The rebuilding of this class with 2A boilers and double chimneys, over the twelve year period from 1943 to 1955, certainly prolonged their lifespan beyond the expected thirty years but their original frames were certainly feeling their age by the 1960's and the class tended to have a reputation as 'rough riders' during the final years they were working. Witness the heaps of mobile scrap sent to the G.C. at Annesley in 1963! I did.

Passing through Crewe on Thursday 15th August 1963, I managed to get a shot of BR Standard Cl.2 No.78030 in the employ of the Civil Engineer and hauling his saloon (they were favoured engines for this type of work where tender first running could take up most of the shift). The engine is stationary at the north end of Crewe station, with a conflab taking place around the engine's midriff. I have no idea what the discussion was about but I'm sure that the connecting rod may have been amongst the various topic's being spoken about. At the time the Cl.2 was a Crewe North engine, and had been since April 1956 when it had transferred from Preston, its first shed. No.78030 transferred again in October 1964 but only down the line to South shed from where it was withdrawn in October 1965. In the background is the 1865 portion of North shed which would see its own centenary on the year of its closure.

My next trip to Crewe works took place in October 1963, Sunday the 13th to be exact, courtesy of the RCTS of which I was then a member. This was no ordinary works visit whereby you waited at the gate with permit in hand, the gate opens at a given time and the guide checks the permit, especially for forgeries - it was easier to get into Wembley for the FA Cup Final I'm sure - anyway, that done there was that seemingly endless walk to the main works site which when you got there made it all seem worth it. The trouble was you didn't know where to look or even begin but the guide was in charge and, believe it or not, he took you through every yard and shop so that everything on works could be seen but you still had to be vigilant otherwise you might miss something. This was no summer Sunday afternoon stroll through a flowery park, this was Olympic standard walking to what seemed, sometimes, like marathon distances - the place was big by any industrial standards. However, none of that on this visit, well none of the first bit anyway because we entered the works in style - by rail. The RCTS Nottingham branch had chartered a train to take us all to firstly Crewe works and then to Horwich works with 'Crab' No.42896 as motive power. So on this date I have only pictures of the works area to show you as we did not do any of the sheds - one has to sacrifice something. On the Erecting shop yard was this BR Standard 9F, No.92002, which had just undergone a heavy repair prior to returning to traffic at Tyseley shed. This engine was one of the first 9F's turned out from Crewe in 1954 and was still, by steam locomotive standards, fairly young. However, its lifespan would in the end be quite short as it had only four more years left before it was withdrawn at Birkenhead shed, its last depot. Whilst steam repairs were still in full swing, Crewe was building diesel locomotives and had been since about 1957 when they started pushing out some of the ubiquitous 350 h.p. 0-6-0 diesel electric shunting locomotives. Of the whole class of what became BR Class 08, Crewe produced about 135 which pales against the much larger numbers turned out from Derby and Darlington. Crewe tended to build the larger main line diesels and during October 1963 they were finishing off the last of a batch of 'Western' class diesel hydraulics for the Western Region, D1030-34 and D1069-73. At the same time a start was being made on the first of a couple of hundred of Brush Type 4 diesel electric's which were built there.

Because Crewe works was such a vast place, it had to employ a large number of locomotives to move engines and materials about the place. Of course on a Sunday these CW allocated engines would be quiet having a rest day. During October 1963 a least five 'Jinties', including No.47658, were part of the allocation. This one continued working here until the summer of 1966 and was withdrawn in September. It was scrapped by Cohen's at Kettering during 1967.

Stabled alongside the boiler park, note the scrapping process in full swing on the right, were a couple more of the Crewe works shunters, Nos.47597 and 43957. Of the latter type, the ex Midland 4F, there was a least five active in the works during late 1963. It seems ironic that Crewe should be using Derby designs for their requirements. Still, ex Lancashire & Yorkshire 0-6-0's had been used until recent times as were former Caledonian railway saddletanks. Perhaps the management weren't too fussy about what they used as long as the job was done. On the left can be seen part of our train which was suitably embellished with carriage headboards.

Amongst the 'scrappers' was this ex LNWR G2a 0-8-0 No.49104 which had been laid up at Northampton for a year, since its November 1962 condemnation, before being called into Crewe for cutting up. By this time the once numerous former LNWR 0-8-0's were down to five survivors, the last of which, Nos.49361 and 49430 would just outlast the Stanier Pacific's by a few weeks.

Outside the Paint shop 9F No.92047 and Cl.5 No.44708 stand out in the sunshine with a unidentified Standard CL5 behind. All three had just completed Heavy Generals overhauls and would be back in traffic within the week assuming no unforeseen hitches showed themselves. New in February 1955, 92047 had spent eight years at Bidston working the John Summers iron ore traffic, between Birkenhead docks and Shotton steel works, before moving to Birkenhead shed in January 1963 and from where it carried on doing much the same job up to withdrawal in November 1967. Whilst employed on the iron ore trains to Shotton, the Bidston 9F's were only attaining about twelve to thirteen thousand miles a year, less than the average family car, whereas most other 9F's were completing three times that mileage. It was actually anticipated that certain members of the class, whilst employed on specific traffic patterns, should have attained in excess of 70,000 miles per annum but the traffic was being either eroded by road transport or being snatched away by the growing fleet of diesels and so the foreseen utilisation never occurred. Bidston shed, which had a small complement of these engines on its books, closed in February 1963. The Class 5, which was only seven years older than the 2-10-0, was BR built at Horwich in October 1948. Its first shed was Crewe North, then in March 1949 it moved to Holyhead only to be reallocated to Chester a month later. During the next August it went to Preston and managed a year of work there before heading off to Springs Branch shed at Wigan for a few weeks before moving on to Edge Hill where it stayed until May 1953. In that month it went back to Crewe North and at the end of the summer timetable it found a more permanent home at Patricroft. In November 1964 it went to its last shed at the nearby former CLC shed at Trafford Park where it found employment until Christmas 1967. After the festive period it was laid up and then withdrawn in January, just predating the shed's demise by a few months. Its final resting place was Cohen's scrapyard at Kettering where it was cut up in February 1969.

If permits for the sheds or works could not be organised, and it was especially difficult to get a weekday permit, it was always a pleasure to sit on the platforms ends at the station and watch the endless traffic movements. Thursday 13th August 1964 was a typical weekday with a great variety of traffic and light engine movements although by now all the important Anglo-Scottish express passenger trains were in the hands of diesels, unless a failure brought one of the rapidly dwindling number of Stanier Pacifics out of North shed. Most of the freight traffic from the Glasgow, Liverpool and Manchester routes, and their northbound counterparts, avoided the station by using the low level tunnels which passed beneath North Junction and it was maddening not to be able to see what was heading these trains. However, goods traffic from the Chester and North Wales direction did not have access to the tunnels and had to traverse the junction at the station and it was one such train, composed of empty iron ore hoppers headed by Stanier 8F No.48065, which I managed to photograph as it came off the Chester line and joined the southbound main line through the station. The 2-8-0 was one of the Vulcan Foundry built examples supplied to the LMS in 1936. Note the star on the cab side indicating this was one of the 8F's specially balanced for working express goods trains. Its first shed was Canklow where it arrived in November. After eighteen years there it moved to Hasland in November 1954 and then, in September 1962 to Burton shed. Its last shed was Leicester to where it transferred in March 1965. Withdrawal came in February 1966 and it was sold to Cashmores of Great Bridge in May of that year. The electrification catenary had been in place here since about 1960 when the Manchester route was electrified and thereby taking away another source of steam power in exchange for the blue electric traction which replaced it. Note the plaque on the nearest catenary pylon has the legend G.158. 97 which was an indication that it was the 97th pylon after milepost 158 on the Glasgow route - just thought I would mention it in passing.

70048
G
158
97

(opposite) From virtually the same vantage point and a little later in the afternoon when the August sun decided to show its face, I copped Willesden based 'Britannia' No.70048 THE TERRITORIAL ARMY 1908-1958 coming off North shed and making its way to the south end of the station to take over a London bound working. Within weeks of this photograph being taken the Pacific would leave London and migrate northwards to Carlisle, first to Kingmoor in October, then to Upperby in November. In December 1966 it moved back to Kingmoor and worked its last from there being withdrawn in May 1967. This engine had certainly been around the sheds during its short life. When new in July 1954 its was sent to Holyhead. Just over five years later it went to Crewe North and then a month later, in December 1959, it started working from Camden for a few weeks before moving to Newton Heath for a one year and eight month stint on the Manchester - Glasgow services. Neasden was next on its list, along with 70049, and from September 1961 to June 1962 both worked the Great Central route. Obviously liking that easy route so much the pair continued working it but from Annesley shed for a further four months. Both went to Willesden in October 1962 in exchange for some clapped 'Royal Scots' which Annesley had to make do with (although Annesley men could basically drive anything - see also Railways North from Nottingham). Back to 70048 which by December had gone to Llandudno Junction shed and after a week their it went further afield to Holyhead. In April of the following year it returned to England stopping off at Aston for eight months before moving back to Willesden.

A view across part of the North junction at Crewe in August 1964 with Stanier Pacific No.46256 SIR WILLIAM A.STANIER F.R.S. making its way onto North shed after bringing in a train from Shrewsbury, in place of a failed diesel. Note the electrification warning stripe across the cab side sheet prohibiting the engine's use south of Crewe 'under the wires' on the main line to London. By now the steam allocation at North shed was diminishing and the few remaining Stanier Pacifics had very little work left. In less than a month all the survivors but one, 46256, would be condemned. No.46256's turn came on 3rd October when it was not quite thirteen years old. Being the only 'Duchess' at Crewe North takes us back to another time during the war years, from May 1943 to mid-April 1944, when only one of the class was allocated here, 6234 DUCHESS OF ABERCORN, one of the four 'Duchesses' up to that time which was built without streamlining. The rest of the class were divided between Polmadie (9) and Camden (19). However, No.6234 did have all but one of the 'Princess Royal' class to keep it company, along with 26 'Royal Scots', 21 'Jubilees', 13 'Patriots', 37 Class 5's, 11 4-4-0's including four compounds, and eight 2-6-4T's. By the end April new construction at the works had brought another Pacific to the shed and by the end of the war the allocation of the premier LMS motive power was being balanced out to cope with the peacetime traffic.

70024
VULCAN

(opposite) With its headcode lamps yet to be put in place, 'Britannia' No.70024 VULCAN stands at the head of what was probably a London-Windermere express in August 1964. It moved to Holyhead shed in September before returning to Crewe North in February 1965. This engine was new from Crewe in October 1951 and went to the Western Region, first to Laira shed in Plymouth and then Cardiff Canton in December 1956, hence the smoke deflectors with cut-outs rather than the original handrails. Aston shed had it twice after it had left the WR, once from September 1961 until it moved to Rugby in October 1962, and again in February 1963 until it went to Willesden two months later. 5A got it in November 1963 and it was during that residency when this photograph was taken. It left Crewe North for good in May 1965 just as the shed was closing down but it only went to South shed. Llandudno Junction got it a year later but only for a couple of months until it went back to Crewe. Carlisle and the rest of the class beckoned in August 1966 but instead of going to Kingmoor it worked for four months from Upperby. For the last year of its short life it was allocated to Kingmoor and was withdrawn in December 1967.

A daily occurrence at Crewe, including some Sunday's, was the coming and going of engines to and from the works. Some steam locomotives would go in and never come out whilst others reappeared after about a month, repaired, repainted and ready for another hundred thousand miles or so in traffic. On 13th August 1964 these two engines, Stanier 4P No.42663 and Cl.5 No.45425, were two of the lucky ones having received major repairs and new shiny black, though unlined paint jobs. The pair were making their way to South shed where for a few days, or longer if necessary, they would be run-in from there prior to returning to their home sheds. Which in the case of the 2-6-4T was Stoke where it had started its working life in 1942 after being built at Derby. Between then and 1964 it had been allocated to a few other sheds including Bangor, Springs Branch and Willesden. With dieselisation and electrification taking over at Stoke it moved to Carnforth in August 1965 then to Edge Hill in January 1966. By the end of the year it was at Trafford Park but a February 1967 move to Birkenhead did not save it from withdrawn in the March, still it must have been due a major repair by then. The Class 5 was heading back to Springs Branch and it too would soldier on until 1967. Throughout its life since new from Armstrong Whitworth in October 1937 it had been associated with just three Lancashire sheds which formed a triangle - Preston 10/37 to 6/38, 9/38 to 10/39, 4/40 to 7/51; Patricroft 6/38 to 9/38, 7/51 to 1/52; Springs Branch 10/39 to 4/40, 1/52 to 10/67 and withdrawal.

Sunday 27th March 1966 was a rather wet day and I tended to concentrate my photography on views inside the Erecting shop and once again 9F No.92002 was the subject but this time in a greater state of undress. By the looks of things it was being stripped down and got ready to receive another boiler but there was still nearly two and a half years left before the abolition of steam on BR so its seems perfectly plausible now to expend so much on steam locomotive repairs. At the time, when everyone knew that the end was so near, it seemed ludicrously wasteful.

Undergoing what was apparently the last major steam repair on that date in March 1966, 'Britannia' No.70038 ROBIN HOOD is without wheels and boiler cladding. 70038 returned to traffic at Kingmoor shed but was withdrawn and sold for scrap in August 1967.

Class 5 No.44659 was being given a somewhat lesser repair concerning cylinder cladding and some new boiler cladding. Whatever was involved, it kept the engine in traffic for another fifteen months. Built at Crewe and released to traffic at Saltley shed in May 1949, it managed fourteen years there before moving on to Leicester. Later that year, in November, Derby got it and they kept hold of it for two years before it went to Colwick to help in the Midlandisation of that shed. Within five months it was off on its travel's again, this time to Aintree where it worked out its last year.

One thing about the rain, once you have dodged the downpour, is that it leaves a sheen on locomotives which in many cases makes them look clean. Ex-Crosti 9F No.92026 of Birkenhead shed didn't need the rain as it had just received a coat of black paint after repair. Its not everyday you see pictures of clean Crosti's, ex, or otherwise.

Stanier 8F No.48037 was in a bit of a state during March 1966, which was not surprising as it had been condemned in the previous December with serious accident damage. In the April following my visit it was hauled to Cashmore's Great Bridge yard and put out of its misery.

Undergoing a steam test, 'Britannia' No.70003 was minus its JOHN BUNYAN nameplates by March 1966 but it had at least received the railless smoke deflectors in accordance with a decade old directive. This Pacific had the shortest allocation history in the class with just four sheds under its belt from new in March 1951 to condemnation in March 1967. The four sheds were Stratford, Norwich from January 1959, March from September 1961 and Kingmoor from December 1963. In the background can be seen the Paint shop with a couple of those diesels outside.

In another elongated bout of misery, the sole BR Standard 8P No.71000 DUKE OF GLOUCESTER was withdrawn on 24th November 1962 with a view to preservation in the National Collection. But after nearly five years of storage at Crewe (notice the nameplates still attached in this March 1966 view outside the Paint shop) it underwent major surgery in 1967 when its left hand cylinder and Caprotti valve gear was removed and later placed in the Science museum at Kensington. The rest of the locomotive was sold for scrap and luckily Woodham's at Barry put in the best tender. Obviously if one of the 'hungrier' yards - and there was plenty of those in 1967 - had got hold of it, we would probably have never found out about the 'dodgy' drawings which, when re-interpreted, eventually changed our whole outlook on what was looked upon then as a fairly ordinary locomotive with a big appetite for coal. The rest since then of course is history.

We end this last visit to Crewe works on a somewhat brighter note than the one when we started some pages back. It wasn't all doom for redundant steam locomotives which entered the works premises. No.71000 would, as we now know, have the last laugh even though it was cast aside by authority. On the other hand Stanier Pacific, No.46235 CITY OF BIRMINGHAM was purchased by its namesake city whilst it was still intact and then eventually it received a cosmetic paint job, as here in the Paint shop on 27th March 1966, with some mechanical remedial work which would be enough for its intended new role in life as a museum piece. This engine was one of the least travelled, allocation wise, of the English based 'Duchesses' having started life at Crewe North in July 1939, being moved to Longsight for storage in September and later that month to Rugby for the same reason. On 3rd October it was back in business and working from Camden shed where it spent the greater part of the war. In May 1944 it moved back to Crewe North where for the next twenty years, until withdrawn on 12th September 1964, it plied the WCML notching up well over one million miles. Note the northlight roof of the shop which allowed an even light throughout the day with no glare - ideal conditions for painting and photography. To the right is one, probably D1993, of the numerous Brush Type 4 diesel locomotives churned out by Crewe from 1964 to 1967.

On 27th March 1966 I visited South shed for the last time and managed a couple of photographs before heading home. By now this place was the only operational steam shed at Crewe and it was the farthest south on the WCML that any steam locomotives could officially work to. Originally the shed itself contained twelve covered through roads but when BR rebuilt the place in the late 1950's it was contracted to cover only the eight roads on the east side and the other four were left open to the elements. From new in October 1945, Stanier Class 5 No.44900 had spent the whole of its life working from Kingmoor shed and would have come visited Crewe occasionally but on this date it had just come the works which normally would have been unusual because Kingmoor's engines went to St Rollox works in Glasgow for repairs, however, that establishment was being modernised to repair only diesel locomotives hence the need for this 4-6-0 to attend Crewe.

A parting shot of a couple of the Crewe South allocation at the south end of the shed in March 1966. The 'Jinty', No.47590 was working out its last year and would be withdrawn before Christmas. 5B had, up to about 1962, a couple of dozen of these useful 0-6-0T's for working the various shunting and pilot jobs around the station and goods yards although much of the work in the goods yards was covered by a similar numbered allocation of first generation diesel shunters which had been at Crewe since LMS days. Cl.5 No.45493 was another ex works engine having received repairs which would take it into 1968 - just. Based then at Banbury (I photographed 45493 on 9th July 1966 arriving at Bournemouth and again on 11th July at Southampton when it was returning north, presumably having spent Sunday on 71B shed), 45493 moved on to Shrewsbury shed when Banbury closed in October 1966. From Salop it moved north, the only escape route for steam, to Kingmoor in March 1967 and was withdrawn in January 1968, ending up at Draper's scrapyard in Hull by Spring. Built at Derby in 1943, the 4-6-0 was first allocated to Longsight in January 1944 and in October 1946 it moved to Crewe North, moving to South shed two years later. In July 1949 it went to Monument Lane for a couple of months before going on to Rugby for a fourteen year residency after which it went to Holyhead in June 1963. In November 1964 it was allocated to Bescot before moving down to Banbury in September 1965. Crewe South shed was closed on 6th November 1967 and was demolished soon afterwards signalling the end of steam in one of the greatest of the British railway centres.

Buxton was one of those sheds which could not be visited at just any time of the year because of its geographical position and height above sea level which meant that it was prone, between November and April, to snow storms and blizzards which invariably blocked the town off from the rest of the world. Of course there was always the railway but even the two routes connecting Buxton with the rest of the network could sometimes be blocked by deep drifts. A visit on Wednesday 8th March 1967 was therefore chancing it somewhat but the forecast must have been favourable – I can't really remember that far back. Anyway the visit, so late in the latter days of steam, was worthwhile even though the sun was spasmodic and weak at times, bright at others, but it was still very cold. This view of Ivatt Cl.2 No.46484 passing the engine shed with a short freight, working in from the Manchester direction, gives a good view of the empty shed yard. The goods sidings are full of wagons carrying limestone, coal and even some oil tanks. An 8F can be seen shunting and, in the background, high above the centre of the spa town, can be seen the viaduct taking the line to Harpurhill. The engine shed still had twelve months of steam activity before closure on 4th March 1968.

Inside the engine shed was J94 Austerity 0-6-0T No.68012, one of two such engines working the Cromford & High Peak line (No.68006 was the other J94 and it was active - just - at Middleton Top). Hunslet built No.68012 arrived at Buxton shed in June 1964 after a BR career which had seen it working either in the Manchester area or in the Peak District. Its LNER career had started at Immingham in July 1946 after it was purchased from the Ministry of Supply. A regular on the C&HP line, it was fitted with oval buffers and, with No.68006, was the first in the class to have a bunker extension. When the section of the C&HP which they worked closed in April 1967, 68006 was withdrawn but 68012 here went to Westhouses shed so that it could work Williamthorpe Colliery in place of the ageing exLMS 0-6-0T No.47313. Its eventual withdrawal in October 1967 meant the end of the class, although many more of its ilk were still working for the National Coal Board and would be for a number of years.

Ex Crosti boilered 9F No.92024 of Birkenhead shed, but was still showing a painted 12A Carlisle Kingmoor shed code, was the only 2-10-0 about Buxton shed on that cold March day in 1967. The deplorable external appearance of the engine was typical of a Birkenhead locomotive; cleaners it seems were non-existent on the Wirral but morale amongst the shed staff must also have been taking a bashing. Anyway 92024 had left Kingmoor shed not far off two years previously, in July 1965. Somebody has removed the front numberplate so perhaps the shed code was painted on otherwise that also would have gone I feel. The 9F worked until the following November when it was condemned and later sold to Campbell's scrapyard at Airdrie, the graveyard of at least thirty other 9F's.

Ivatt Cl.2 No.46485 was one of a batch of these useful engines which would work out their last days from Buxton shed. On shed that day were 46402, 46465 (withdrawn), 46480, 46492 and, joining later, 46484. Others were out and about and made up the complement to around a dozen. Although some were long term residents, others had lately come from Newton Heath, Springs Branch and even Aston. By July all would have been condemned and sold for scrap. Other residents that day included three 8F's, one withdrawn, one down for repair and one active.

QUEENS

(opposite) Saturday 15th June 1968, only weeks away from the ending but still the North West of England could put on a good show of steam motive power and Manchester (Victoria) was one of the venues for seeing some action. Here on one of the through roads are three Stanier Class 5's, numbered front to rear as 44780, 45206 and 45076. Their job to bank trains up Miles Platting bank be they passenger or freight, steam or diesel. As a train passed them one of the trio would peel off, join the same road and chase the train up the bank, usually catching up within a hundred yards. At the top of the incline the banker would slow allowing the train to accelerate away. When a path was available the banker would drift back down to Victoria, steam past his comrades and then and then rejoin the queue. In days gone by this job was usually entrusted to a couple of Newton Heath's ex Lancashire & Yorkshire 0-6-0 tender engines but now, with most other classes of ex LMS steam locomotive either extinct or on the point of, the '5's' have got the job along with most others at this time. For the record, all were on this particular date Newton Heath engines. No.44780 came from Springs Branch in December 1967 and was withdrawn at the end of June. No.45206 came to Newton Heath from Fleetwood in July 1965 and in July of this year went over to Rose Grove to join the others. No.45076 had spent all of its working life on the old Central Division and was only ever allocated to three sheds Bolton, Farnley Junction and Newton Heath. It to succumbed at the end of June.

On the following Saturday I captured Bolton 8F No.48319 galloping through Victoria and heading for the bottom of Miles Platting bank with a van train. Sure enough, as soon as the last vehicle had passed, Cl.5 No.44910 the banker, chased after the train to give it a push. This twenty-four year old 2-8-0 was well travelled. Built at Crewe, it went to Perth in January 1944. After war's end it returned to England and Rose Grove in October 1946. April 1949 saw it move south to Saltley and five years later it went to Barrow Hill but within three months had settled in at Toton for a nine year stay. Nottingham had it for a few months in 1963 before it came north to Fleetwood in November. It was allocated to Springs Branch in February 1966 and then in December 1967 it went to Patricroft and a few weeks later to Heaton Mersey. Bolton got it in May and it was withdrawn a week after this photograph was taken.

Shunting Manchester (Exchange) station on 15th June 1968 was another Cl.5, No.45156 AYRSHIRE YEOMANRY. The Patricroft based engine was another that got to Rose Grove shed in July, ready for the mass extinction of August. Note the nameplate, or lack thereof. Whenever the nameplate and the plaque was removed, somebody at either Edge Hill shed from where it had come from to get to Patricroft, or somebody at Patricroft had decided to paint a reasonable copy of the original. At a distance it appears to have the plate but closer inspection reveals a good paint job. Whether the nameplate/plates and plaques were taken off officially or otherwise I would be interested to know so please write via the Publisher and I will reply. Also if anybody knows where or who the artist was I would be grateful for the information.

Going back in time now to Sunday 13th October 1963. Venue: Horwich works and the second stage of the RCTS special trip from Nottingham via Crewe works. As will be seen from the pictures, the weather turned out glorious and the late afternoon sun was perfectly placed. 'Crab' No.42890 was not perfectly placed as it was in the scrapyard and would be Monday morning's first job. Note that everything on the engine is still in place, numberplate, shedplate and the complete motion - not bad considering it had been withdrawn five months previously. Its last shed was Gorton, where it would have been fairly secure and souvenir hunters were actively discouraged. 42890 was built at Crewe in 1930 as LMS No.13190 and spent the next seventeen years working from sheds on the LMS Western Division such as the two Crewe depots, Longsight, Willesden, Nuneaton and Edge Hill. In May of 1947 it moved to the Midland Division to work at Saltley, Burton and Kettering. Gorton got it in June 1961 and the rest is history. It seemed a little disconcerting at the time but sister engine No.42896 had brought us from Nottingham and would return us home. In the event the trip went without a hitch until we got to Beeston when it burst into flames between the frames. However, on arrival at the Midland station the flames were soon extinguished and our 'Crab' went back to its shed at Nottingham, later moving before withdrawal in March 1965.

Just in front of 42890 was Horwich works shunter No.11324 which appears to have been left on the scrap road with a view to it being broken up. I'm not sure of its disposition at that time and it may well have been left there for the weekend but I have a feeling that the former Lancashire & Yorkshire 0-6-0ST was condemned at sometime near the date of our visit. Certainly sister engine 11368 was not active, and No.11304 had already disappeared whereas No.11305, the last active member of the class, was in the stabling shed used by these Service locomotives.

One engine certainly getting the chop was Fowler LMS 4F No.44444, a Crewe product of 1927, which had been stripped of boiler lagging and a few other bits during Saturday overtime. This 0-6-0 had been withdrawn in August from Springs Branch shed and took the convenient, somewhat short, trip from Wigan to Horwich. What price that numberplate today I wonder - has somebody got it and where is it? The different classes of locomotive cut up here during the last ten years of steam on BR, was quite interesting, not just the former L&Y types but also ex LNER engines which had been sent by Gorton works during 1962 as operations at that place wound down. A list of what was cut up here during the period from 1958 onwards would be worth seeing, if such a document exists. Meanwhile we can only look at what went when we were there.

42973

(opposite) Stanier mogul No.42973 was in works for repair or so it would seem, note the stencilled numbers applied to different parts of the engine, a normal routine at many works, however, later in the month the 2-6-0 was suddenly condemned and then cut up by the Horwich demolition squad. Note the narrow gauge track (1' 6") alongside the engine, remnants of the days when 0-4-0ST WREN and sisters used to transport materials about the works. Latterly a little 0-4-0 diesel, ZM 32 was doing the job with the steam locomotive enjoying retirement. Getting back to No.42973, this engine was allocated to Nuneaton shed and like most of the class visited Horwich for maintenance. Another Nuneaton mogul, No.42976 had recently visited for overhaul, was condemned in August and cut up before our visit. No.42984 from Crewe South had a similar experience, being condemned in September and never again leaving the works. The next to arrive was Stoke's No.42949 which was condemned in November and cut up in January 1964. One wonders sometimes what was going through the minds of the authorities during the transition years of the early 1960's. For instance, every new diesel locomotive delivered had the potential of displacing at least two steam locomotives from the same work. But, reliability was still something of a problem with some classes of diesel so 'tread carefully' was perhaps the order of the day. Two other facts to throw into consideration, BR was losing goods traffic at an alarming rate and the thirty year life expectancy of a steam locomotive was a good guide, as in the case of 42973, to retire certain locomotives. No matter what we as enthusiasts think about the wholesale withdrawals and condemnations of that period, there is no doubt that BR wanted desperately to modernise their image and it appears that cost did not come into it. Also, many of the BR management involved are now no longer with us so our questions will remain unanswered. Official documents exist but they do not always tell either the whole story or the truth as to how directives were interpreted. It was certainly a wasteful period in the least but then post-war austerity was over and the consumer orientated 1960's beckoned.

One locomotive which had just arrived in works for repair, and as we now know, was assured a dignified departure was double-chimneyed 'Jubilee' No.45596 BAHAMAS. Its tender appears to be in a somewhat unhealthy state with the underframe on one wagon and the body on another. just why it was in this condition escapes me now but at that time such a state could easily have been terminal but Stockport Edgeley based 45596 was repaired and put back into traffic until July 1966 when it was withdrawn and later preserved. This was one of the North British Loco. Co. built 'Jubilees', coming into traffic in January 1935. For the next three years it worked from Western Division sheds but in September 1938 moved to the Midland Division where, at sheds such as Kentish Town, Millhouses and Bristol, it served through the war years. In September 1947 it returned to the Western Division and before moving to 9B in July 1962 had been at Upperby since 1956. Note on the right our trusty Nottingham 'Crab' which returned us home via the former L&Y route through the Pennines and Summit tunnel.

This little gem is an ex L&Y Barton Wright 0-4-4T, one of the handful of such engines used for carriage heating and stationery boiler duties at various locations on the old L&Y system such as Blackpool Central, Manchester Red Bank carriage sidings and other places. Every so often, about every ten years or so, these SB's had to visit Horwich for necessary maintenance and they would bring with them their tall chimney extensions, seen here strapped to the right side of the boiler and poking into the spectacle of the cab. S that it was impossible for them to move under their own power, the cranked driving axle was removed making it in essence an 0-2-4T. It would have been given a stationary boiler number by both the LMS and BR but I'm not sure what that was or where its usual home was. I wonder why none of these were preserved?

Lostock Hall shed was amongst the last of the working steam sheds on BR. On 15th June 1968, two months prior to the final day, the place was packed with both working and redundant locomotives. Mainly Stanier Cl.5's and 8F's, it was still nice to see, hear and sense so much hot metal. Showing their smokeboxes to the camera are, left to right, 8F's Nos.48294 and 48493, and Cl.5 No.45212. All lasted out to August. No.48294 was one of the thirty-nine ex War Department engines (No.70443) which became BR property in 1949, and started its BR career at Crewe South in October 1949, and arriving at Lostock Hall in May 1968 from Edge Hill. It was sold for scrap to T.W.Ward at Beighton. No.48493 was built in July 1945 at Horwich. This engine was a visitor from Rose Grove and it had arrived at that shed in May 1968 from Speke Junction. It too went to Ward's at Beighton. No.45212 had come to Lostock Hall in January 1968 from Kingmoor. It is now preserved.

This view of the withdrawn line at Lostock Hall on 15th June 1968 gives an idea of what was to become of all those engines condemned in August. Stanier 8F's and Cl.5's have had their tenders cleared out and are ready for the journey to their respective scrap merchants. The sleepered ground was once the depots coal stack but now it is just a dump. After closure, and when all this mobile metal had been taken away, the engine shed became home for the Area Civil Engineer's plant maintenance department.

Vandalised and looking in a very sorry state, Ivatt mogul No.43027 was one of three of the class at Lostock Hall that June day in 1968. Withdrawn in May, the 2-6-0 had come to the depot in January 1968 from Workington. It ended its days at the scrapyard of Arnott Young in Dinsdale.

The southern end of Preston station, 22nd June 1968, with Stanier Cl.5 No.44874 of Carnforth shed approaching from the south. The two signal gantries would eventually give way to colour light signalling as the West Coast Main Line electrification spread northwards to Glasgow but that was still about six years off. Gone now are all the Pacific's which headed the Anglo-Scottish passenger traffic with train names such as *THE ROYAL SCOT, THE CALEDONIAN, THE ROYAL HIGHLANDER.* In 1968 the London to Glasgow, and northwards passenger traffic was in the hands of the English Electric Type 4 Co-Co's (Class 50) which had taken over from the older Type 4's from the same stable (Class 40). The newer locomotives were a 'stopgap' measure to speed up the passenger expresses until electrification of the route north of Weaver Junction was carried out. But steam locomotives concerned me today and it was a matter of photograph what you could and more importantly where because by now the little enclaves of steam were basically disappearing at an alarming rate. Lostock Hall, Rose Grove and Carnforth engine sheds had become Mecca's to the enthusiasts and not a weekend went by without thousands of us doing our pilgrimage's for what at any time could be the last occasion.

Newly arrived at Lostock Hall shed, Fairburn 2-6-4 Cl.4 tank No.42287 stands in the old East Lancs. side of Preston station at the head of a Liverpool bound stopping train on Tuesday 13th July 1965. In the background can be seen the main line section of the station angling off to the south, Preston No.3 signal box controlled that part of the station, whilst these platforms put trains on an easterly direction at first. No.42287's route would take it along the Blackburn line for a couple of miles to Todd Lane Junction whence it would take the westerly route past Lostock Hall engine shed and over the WCML at Farington and then on to Ormskirk. This engine would not stay in the area and moved to Trafford Park in October for a one year stay after which it went to its final shed at Wakefield from where it was withdrawn in June 1967 just twenty years old. This Derby built tank engine started its working life at Newton Heath in 1947 where, after twelve years it moved across Manchester to Agecroft. July 1960 found it at Lees beginning a three year residency after which it went to Rugby and after two years there on to Willesden in April 1965. Unwanted, it moved back north to Lostock Hall and that is how this picture was captured.

Staying at the East Lancs. platforms on that Tuesday in July 1965, another Liverpool bound 'stopper' was headed by one of Bank Hall's BR Standards, Cl.4 No.75048, a twelve year old which looked thoroughly unkempt but was going to be amongst the last ones at Carnforth in august 1968.

Lostock Hall BR Standard Cl.2 No.78041 was on station pilot duties at Preston on 13th July 1965. From new in December 1954 until its June 1964 move to Lostock Hall, it had been at Bank Hall shed in Liverpool. Withdrawal came in May 1967, its thirteenth year.

Rose Grove was an unlikely name for a motive power depot but that was the name given to this former Lancashire & Yorkshire Railway engine shed nestling on the western outskirts of Burnley. If anybody had asked me in, say 1958, "Which is going to be the last operational steam shed on BR?", then I would most probably not have said Rose Grove. I know that Carnforth was the other depot closed that day - 5th August 1968 - and both places share the distinction but nevertheless this was the last place I would have chosen. Opened in 1899, the place was little changed other than a new roof was necessary in 1947 and that a mechanical coaling plant was installed by the LMS. The motive power had changed over the years too compared to the Stanier locomotives which had to drop their fires in 1968. During World War Two, for instance, there was only five Stanier engines allocated, all 2-6-4T's and these were alongside seven 'Crabs', two Fowler 0-8-0's, two Fowler 0-6-0T's, four exL&Y 0-6-0ST's, eight exL&Y 0-6-0's, six exL&Y 2-4-2T's, and fourteen exL&Y 0-8-0's. A typical allocation of a depot mainly concerned with the movement of freight. Since 1947 more than eighty different Stanier 8F's had been allocated to Rose Grove and of course there was that other great 2-8-0 of the BR period, the WD Austerity of which more than thirty different examples came and went over the 1950's and 60's. Even as late as June 1965 there was still thirteen WD's allocated to Rose Grove. This view on 15th June 1968 has seven Stanier 8F's basking in the sunshine outside the shed, with double that number inside.

A general view of the yard at Rose Grove in July with 8F's predominating. The smoke is off the Lostock Hall allocated diesel shunter which had just started its engine, and was on loan.

Stanier Class 5's were also abundant at Rose Grove during the latter days, with no less that forty-nine different examples having been allocated to the shed since 1955. In June 1968 more than a dozen could be found around the depot at the weekend, although at least half had been withdrawn. No.44690 here was still operational even though its position on the storage line would seem otherwise, however, it would be amongst the casualties of 5th August.

Class 5's Nos.45382 and 45386 were two other 4-6-0's which were still in favour during June. The former had come to Rose Grove in 1966 whilst the latter was one of Lostock Hall's allocation and would return there in time for withdrawal on 4th August.

One 4-6-0 which was not a Stanier design on Rose Grove shed in June 1968 was BR Standard Cl.4 No.75019. This rather immaculate engine was allocated to Carnforth shed and worked on the Grassington branch during the week and carries a shedplate showing what looks suspiciously like 24G which was Skipton. Although officially allocated to Carnforth, 75019 was a favourite for working the Grassington branch but for some peculiar reason this was worked from Rose Grove! The engine could also be found on occasions shunting Skipton goods yard. Did some wag there substitute a 24G shedplate? This is another engine which worked to the end but it was not a candidate for preservation and was scrapped at Campbell's in Airdrie by the end of the year.

This 8F will not be needing that miniature snowplough any more. Rose Grove 15th June 1968.

A problem with its motion was obviously 8F No.48384's reason for condemnation. Note the big painted X on the tender (a Gorton works symbol for "scrap it"). The depot's diesel shunter has just taken the 2-8-0 off the shed's front yard and is now pushing it over the turntable and into a siding to await the scrap merchants agent.

8F No.48115 was condemned in July 1968 but in this 15th June photograph it is still in traffic and is simply resting here alongside the shed at Rose Grove. This was an LMS built engine which came from Crewe works in March 1939, its first shed being Warwick. It came from Heaton Mersey to Rose Grove just three weeks before this view of it was captured, and was already in a sorry and tired state. The south wall of the engine shed gives us some clues as to the rebuilding of this shed from its original northlight roof days. Immediately behind the engine is the second portion of the rebuilding, where concrete fabrications were used to finish a job which had been disrupted by the war, prior to which a straight pitch roof with vent was put over each road but only for about three quarters of the length of the shed.

No.48773 was an 8F of many identities and nearly as many lives as a cat. Starting life as LMS No.8233, it was seconded to the War Department and became WD307 then later WD70307. It number was changed yet again by the WD to 500. BR got it back and put it into traffic at Polmadie shed as No.48773. In December 1962 it was withdrawn but was reinstated the following January. However, in June it was withdrawn yet again but was once again reinstated during October and sent to Kingmoor depot. Making its way south in January 1964 it got to Stockport Edgeley for a six month spell before climbing the hill to Buxton for the summer season. In September it reallocated to Bolton for a four year stay and got to Rose Grove during the last full month of steam working. On the shed yard on 13th July 1968 it has acquired a cab stripe. Withdrawn with all the rest in August, it was later preserved and occasionally takes on its former LMS identity.

8F No.48400 was one of the Great Western built engines put together at Swindon works in 1943. Its first shed was Swindon in June and two months later it moved to St Phillips Marsh at Bristol. The engine went to the LMS, at Saltley in November 1946. Four months after Nationalisation it went to Toton and eighteen months later to Stourton until February 1950 when it returned to Toton for a seven year stretch. In February 1957 it moved back into ex GWR territory at Swansea. In August 1959 it was allocated to Llanelly for a five year stay but left there in September 1964 in favour of Lostock Hall. Its first spell at Rose Grove was from February 1966 to May 1967 when Carnforth required its services. Four months later it returned to Rose Grove and is seen on the turntable there on 13th July 1968; it was one of those which lasted to the end. By Christmas 1968 it was in the hands of T.W.Ward at Beighton being recycled.

This 13th July 1968 picture gives a fair idea of what Rose Grove was all about during those final summer months of 1968. Taking centre stage is 8F No.48247 another ex WD engine with a previous identity. When it was on loan to the LMS in 1940/41, it was given LMS No.8227 but on recall to the WD it became 301, then later WD70301. In 1949 it was taken into British Railways stock and given the number it is now wearing. It first BR shed was Crewe South, followed by Birkenhead from April 1950 then, from October 1953, Mold Junction. Speke Junction took it over from August 1959 but only until January 1961 when it moved to Willesden. Three years later it went to Northampton shed until being allocated to Nuneaton shed in August 1965. Carnforth got it in June 1966 and it finally got to Rose Grove in May 1967. It too was withdrawn at the end. No.48340 on the other hand had a much simpler, though no less eventful life. Turned out from Horwich as LMS No.8340 in January 1944, its first

shed was Perth where it resided until August 1946. Crewe South was its next shed and it stayed there until January 1950 when Willesden acquired it. In April 1949 it had spent a month on loan to Northwich and they liked it so much they invited it back in November 1950 when, for the next fifteen years it took part in the daily procession of ICI limestone hopper trains from Northwich to Tunstead and back. Luckily, the return journey was virtually down hill all the way with the loaded hoppers and a tight reign was required - something these engines were good at. Aintree shed had it from April 1965 to June 1967 after which it returned to Northwich to help out with the limestone trains. Rose grove got it for the first time in march 1968 but a month later Bolton called and it went back over there but in July Bolton's days as an engine shed were over and the still useful No.48340 was sent back to Rose Grove for a dignified if somewhat premature withdrawal.

Morecambe (Promenade) station was built by the Midland Railway in their bid to share in the seasonal though lucrative Lancashire seaside traffic. Later the LMS electrified the route between Heysham and Lancaster via Morecambe hence the overhead catenary. Stanier Cl.5 No.45402, of Lostock Hall shed has the Morecambe portion of a London bound train which it would take to Preston to be attached to another portion from either Blackpool or perhaps even Carlisle. Note the d.m.u. in the same platform. This more than likely was on a Leeds service.

The pilot at Promenade station on the day of my visit was Ivatt Cl.2 tank No.41221, a long time resident of Green Ayre shed in Lancaster but not for much longer as it was condemned by the end of the month and sold off for scrap to Motherwell Machinery & Scrap in December.

The west end of the yard at Carnforth on 22nd June 1968 presented six BR 9F's and three Stanier Cl.5's, all redundant. The 2-10-0's have between them a nice mixture of the tenders used by the class - BR1C, BR1F and BR1G. Only the BR1B type and the BR1K, the mechanical stoker type are missing. Note that the tenders are being emptied of their contents as the days ticked by towards the August deadline, this storage area would begin to overflow and but thinning out had begun as engines were taken away to scrap yards near and far. The main line to Barrow leads off to the left.

At the south end of the shed site the mechanical ash and coaling plants offer a temporary refuge on 22nd June 1968 for two of the depot's own stud of Class 5's, Nos.44874 and 44758. We saw 44874 earlier in the day making its way north, light engine, through Preston station. Crewe built in April 1945, this engine was first allocated to Crewe North shed and four years later it went down to Bletchley for an eight month stay before returning the Crewe in February 1950. Three months later it went to Preston and then, in September 1950 it came to Carnforth to enjoy a near eighteen year residency only upset slightly by a one month loan period to Stoke shed in July 1961. It worked to the end of steam and was withdrawn in August. No.44758 was one of the last locomotives built at Crewe under the LMS regime. Its first shed was Perth in September 1947 but it was back in Crewe by December where it resided at North shed for the next twelve years. Springs Branch got it in May 1959 and in June 1960 it was working from Longsight for a few months before moving over to Edge Hill for a couple of years. Making its way north, as if by instinct, Lancaster was its next port of call in June 1962 and after nearly four years there it eventually found its way to Carnforth in April 1966. Not quite making it to the end, it was withdrawn a couple of weeks after my visit.

Making its way off shed at Carnforth on 22nd June 1968, Lostock Hall Cl.5 No.44713 passes between the depot's breakdown train and coal stocks before sliding under the footbridge. The curve of the railway here can be easily made out as it goes into gradual transition from west to south. No.44713 was one of the BR built Cl.5's, emerging from Horwich in November 1948 and proceeding to Crewe North shed. Eighteen months later it moved to Rugby and after six years there, it moved on to Willesden for a couple of years. Crewe South had it from June 1958 until November 1962 when it went south again, but this time to Northampton. In June 1964 it started its migration northwards by going to Chester for three months then its was off to Springs Branch. In another June timed reallocation it went to Lostock Hall in 1967 and was working to the end nearly making its twentieth birthday.

Having passed beneath me, No.44713 continues on through the yard at Carnforth passing further coal stocks and one of the Clayton centre cab diesels which worked in the area for a while in the late 1960's. The expanse of the goods yard on this side of the station can be easily appreciated and the amount of goods traffic appears healthy enough but it was a Saturday and not many goods trains are in transit.

Vulcan Foundry built Stanier Class 5 No.45025 came into traffic in August 1934 with this Mark.1 riveted tender. It kept that type of tender throughout its thirty-four year life. Carnforth engine shed, 22nd June 1968.

Armstrong Whitworth built Stanier Class 5 No.45134 came into traffic in May 1935 with this Mark.2 welded tender. It too kept that same type of tender throughout its thirty-three year life. Carnforth engine shed, 22nd June 1968.

Whereas Rose Grove tended to have a greater proportion of 8F's in the latter months of 1968, Carnforth had a greater proportion of Class 5's on its allocation. On 22nd June 1968 it was nice to view over the still active taper boilers of three Class 5's at the north-west end of Carnforth shed.

Already at Carnforth, on 22nd June 1968, the preserved locomotives which would take over the depot when it became Steamtown, were beginning to congregate. Fairburn 2-6-4T No.42085 was there with Thompson B1 No.61306, the tender of which is visible on the left. In the background the junction station where WCML expresses thundered through and trains for the coast line via Barrow stopped.

A ground level view of the withdrawn 9F's at Carnforth in June 1968. Amongst their number were 92077, 92091, 92118, 92167 and 92223. All had appointments with various scrap merchants.

(opposite) On the afternoon of Saturday 11th July 1964, whilst en route to Scotland by car, I visited Oxenholme where the Windermere branch joins the WCML. Luckily there was still plenty of steam motive power working both the branch and the main line though most of the important Anglo-Scottish traffic was in the hands of diesels. However, some of the 'lesser' expresses were still in the main steam hauled such as the Carlisle-Liverpool which had just stopped to pick up passengers from Kendal and Windermere. Bank Hall 'Jubilee' No.45698 MARS was heading the train and the fireman, with his knotted handkerchief atop his head, leans out of the cab window just as my camera shutter opened. No.45698 was one of a batch of eight new Crewe built 'Jubilees' sent to Newton Heath in 1936 and numbered 5695 to 5702. No.5698 arrived in May 1936 and stayed there until April 1938 when it was called over to Holbeck. six months later it went to Derby but was back at 26A to do war service. In October 1946 it moved over to bank Hall shed and except for the spending the summer months of 1948 at Southport shed, it worked from the old L&Y shed in Liverpool until withdrawn in October 1965.

Shortly after MARS departed for the south, one of Carnforth's Stanier Cl.5's, No.45390 came thundering through on a northbound express/excursion (1L27) composed of some assorted coaching stock, the first two vehicles of which were Eastern Region, most likely of Thompson design riding on Gresley type bogies.

Earlier on, a Manchester (Victoria) to Windermere excursion (1L18) had stopped in the branch platform headed by Newton Heath Cl.5 No.45083. This thirty year old engine had spent much of its early life working from depots in Scotland although its first four years, after being delivered from Vulcan foundry in 1935, were spent at Crewe South shed. In July 1939 it moved north to Edinburgh and Dalry Road shed but after only five months it went to Perth for the duration of WW2. Six months before Nationalisation it came south to Kingmoor, staying at the former Caley shed until August 1962 when it moved across the city to Upperby. May 1963 saw it allocated to Southport and in June 1964 it went to its final shed at Newton Heath. At its withdrawal in December 1967 it was just two months off its thirty-third birthday.

Freights fitted and unfitted, express passenger, semi-fast, stoppers - all were the bread and butter of the mixed traffic Stanier Cl.5's and No.45081 comfortably wheels this northbound freight through Oxenholme on Saturday 11th July 1964 in style. Note the self weighing tender (No.10590) which was attached to this engine from December 1963 to January 1965 when the engine received one of the standard LMS Mk.1 riveted tenders which it kept to withdrawal. Another of the Vulcan Foundry built Cl.5's, No.45081 was delivered to Crewe North shed in March 1935. From late April to early May it was at Bushbury after which it returned to Crewe but to South shed for a couple of months. In August it went back to North shed before moving north to Perth in September. Until November 1944, when it went to Kingmoor, it spent various periods at either St Rollox or Perth. Kingmoor kept it until March 1962 when it moved to Upperby for fifteen months before returning to Kingmoor. In June 1964 it went back to Upperby and stayed there to withdrawal in October 1965. Just beyond the road bridge, on the west side of the line stood Oxenholme engine shed, the one time home for the Windermere branch engines until closure in June 1962, after which time the engines were supplied by Carnforth.

42359

(opposite) Fowler 2-6-4T No.42359 brings a local train off the Windermere branch on that Saturday afternoon in July. When this 1964 holiday season finished the Derby built Fowler tank was stored for a few weeks before withdrawal in October. This engine had been at Carnforth since June 1961 but had previously spent three years there from new in 1930. Between those times it had certainly been around. In October 1933 it moved to Stoke then, in July 1935, it came north again to Barrow where it had twenty-two years working the coastline to Workington and around Morecambe Bay. In October 1957 it reallocated to Willesden for a couple of years and during that time it spent three months working from Neasden shed. Returning northwards yet again, it got as far as Northwich in August 1959 and resided there until coming back to where it all started and was to finish, at Carnforth. When operational Oxenholme shed was home to half a dozen or so 2-6-4 tanks of either the Fowler or Stanier variety, and to finish off the complement, a couple of Fowler 0-6-0T's were allocated.

Later on No.42359 takes a main line working onto the Windermere branch.

How the mighty had fallen. Not only was 'Duchess' No.46254 CITY OF STOKE-ON-TRENT filthy dirty, it was engaged on duties not befitting its status. Saturday 11th July 1964, just two months away from condemnation, the Pacific is working out its final days hauling WCML goods trains. This 300-tons or so load it was bringing down the hill from Tebay would not be taxing it one bit but to see such a locomotive relegated to work such as this was quite sad indeed.

Coming off the branch, Fairburn Cl.4 No.42147, also of Carnforth shed, brings main line stock into Oxenholme station. This engine was a recent acquisition from Lostock Hall having arrived at Carnforth in February. One of the BR Derby built examples of the class, No.42147 had spent all of its previous life working in Lancashire, first at Fleetwood from May 1948 then from February 1950 from Accrington. After just a couple of weeks there it moved over to Lower Darwen shed where it settled down for twelve and a half years. Lostock Hall got it in September 1962 and it was withdrawn in May 1965. By October it was in the hands of Cashmore's at their Great Bridge yard.

For a Saturday there was plenty of goods movement on the WCML and 'Crab' No.42856 has this Up fitted freight nicely in check as it charges through Oxenholme station on 11th July 1964. Birkenhead based, the mogul would be withdrawn during November and sold a Sheffield scrapyard. Note the banner repeater signal on the gantry by the roof indicating the main line signal at the end of the platform is off.

One year later, on 10th July 1965, I returned to Oxenholme but this time the weather was more typical of the British summer and rain somewhat glazed the proceedings. At virtually the same spot where I recorded 'Jubilee' MARS on the Carlisle to Liverpool express, I managed to get a similar view of 'Jubilee' No.45627 SIERRA LEONE, albeit with a painted nameplate, again on the Carlisle-Liverpool express. Even the fireman is obliging with a backward glance. Another Bank Hall loco, No.45627 had been at the shed since March 1962 and would end its days there being withdrawn in September 1966. During its thirty-two year lifetime, this engine had been allocated to thirteen different sheds from Carlisle to London and from Bristol to Sheffield. Note the cab side warning stripe forbidding access to the WCML south of Crewe.

There was even a 'Royal Scot' out on the line on 10th July 1965. Even in its deplorable state, No.46140 THE KING'S ROYAL RIFLE CORPS, still looks impressive as it works hard through Oxenholme station with a train of new motor vehicles on Carflats. Withdrawn in October, Kingmoor based 46140 was the penultimate 'Scot' being outlived only by 46115 SCOTS GUARDSMAN which was withdrawn in December, and subsequently preserved. One of the North British built 'Scots', much of No.46140's life was spent working from WCML sheds with a two year period, from September 1959, working the Midland main line. It went to Kingmoor shed in October 1964 working as here, virtually to the end. It was appropriately scrapped in Scotland, its birthplace, by J.McWilliam's of Shettleston.

Another northbound freight that day had BR 9F No.92249 at its head. By the looks of its a couple of shovelfuls of coal have just been introduced to the firebox and the 2-10-0 leaves a nice exhaust behind.

Further north up the WCML, at the bottom of the notorious Shap bank, was the little village of Tebay, the population of which consisted almost entirely of people employed by the railway. The London & North Western Railway built an engine shed here in 1861 to house banking engines. A joint station was set up when the South Durham & Lancashire Union Railway brought in their line from Kirkby Stephen. In 1867, when the SD&LUR had become part of the North Eastern Railway, the NER built its own four road engine shed to the north of the joint station and on the east side of their line where it branched off the WCML. So, a settlement was created which for the next one hundred years was to be totally dependant on the railways. The NER housed engines here to serve the western end of their line from Darlington whereas the LNWR stabled their engines purely to work the incline up to Shap. By 1948 the former NER shed was long closed with NER, and later LNER, engines using the LNWR and later LMS facilities when necessary although the LNER maintained a turntable and water tank on the site of the old depot until Nationalisation. In this Monday 12th July 1965 view of Tebay Junction, we have Ivatt Mogul No.43035 coming off the Down WCML line and entering the former LMS shed yard. The WCML, with its rising gradient discernible, takes centre stage with the signal box looking over it and the ex LNER Kirkby Stephen line going off to the right. The bridge parapet marks the spot where the WCML crosses the River Lune. No.43035 had been a Tebay engine since January 1957 and when this photograph was taken it had less than four months to work before withdrawal.

Two of Tebay's resident Fairburn 2-6-4 tanks in July 1965 were 42095 and 42225. The former engine was one of the Brighton built batch which went into traffic in June 1951 on the Southern Region at Tunbridge Wells shed. In September of that year it moved to Ashford and worked from there until May 1958 when it was allocated to Dover for just over a year. In September 1959 it went back to Ashford in a bid to get onto the north bank of the Thames. Three months later it managed that getting only as far as Watford but nevertheless on the right lines. In July 1961 in really broke out and travelled 300 miles to Carlisle but arrived at the wrong shed - Canal. In May 1963, fancying a life in the country, it came to Tebay to work the Shap bank which it successfully carried out until June 1966. when it was condemned. No.42225, was not only built in the right place but it worked all of its life on the right side of the Thames. Leaving Derby works as No.2225 in April 1946 it went to work on the London, Tilbury & Southend line first from Plaistow shed and then from May 1952 from Tilbury. It had a slower migration northwards and got to Neasden in April 1954 where it stayed for nearly eight years. then it was off to Saltley and after nine months there it went to Rowsley. Returning to its birthplace in May 1964, it came to Tebay in March 1965, so was the newcomer. Evidence of the 1947 rebuilding of the engine shed can be seen, especially in the area of the roof where concrete troughs took over from the original timbered sections.

Ivatt Cl.4 No.43009 was out of service at the time of my visit to Tebay. It is stabled on the east side of the shed where the original, well built and decorative 1861 wall was kept intact. Note the bricked-up arches where windows once allowed daylight into the place. The gloom did not help photography but luckily I had my tripod and time to execute a good exposure. No.43009 is not looking its best but it still had another year and four months of service before it until withdrawal. This is one of the least travelled locomotives featured in this album and its only other shed since being built at Horwich in 1948 was Workington which it left in September 1960 to come here.

Meet Fairburn 2-6-4T No.42110, the designated banking engine on 12th July 1965. A resident of Tebay since it left Rose Grove in February 1963, this engine had spent the previous fourteen years, since leaving the paint shop at Derby, working from sheds on the old LMS Central Division. Today it is looking rather dirty except for a patch on the tank where I suspect either a leak or overflowing filler cap. The small mechanical coaling plant behind the engine was erected in 1956 and was a useful addition to the depot's facilities. However, closure came in the end to Tebay on 1st January 1968 although diesel locomotives were stabled here for some years afterwards just in case a train stalled on the bank or was desperate for a push.

When I was working at Wilford power station one of my colleagues there had not long past been a locomotive driver at Tebay shed. It is through his kind generosity that included in my collection there is a photograph taken from the footplate of a banking engine just about to attack the bank. The train engine incidently is the Stephenson Link 'Black Five' No.44767 (still with us today). "Thank you Ted." *M.Castledine collection.*

In July 1967, during a trip to Durham and Northumberland where I went to capture on film the last of BR steam before the Region pulled the plug in September, I took a day off and crossed over to Carlisle to see what was happening there. 'Britannia's' seemed to be happening - everywhere. By now all the surviving 'Britannia' population had gathered at Kingmoor, all twenty-seven of them. Their nameplates had been removed but the names themselves had been restored using paint and a lot of patience. I think the staff at Kingmoor were responsible for the restoration and if it was I congratulate them belatedly for giving some dignity back to their charges. Here is No.70010 OWEN GLENDOWER arriving at Citadel from the shed to await its working. On this side of the engine the plate was reading OWEN GLENDOWER whilst the other side was showing OWAIN GLYNDOWER.

With 70010 now stabled on the through road which was the usual waiting area for locomotives taking over southbound workings, No.70022 TORNADO, with a painted front numberplate as well, passes through the station to await the arrival of its train.

TORNADO has backed onto its train and now gets smartly away southbound with another express.

Later in the afternoon No.70038 ROBIN HOOD comes from Kingmoor shed and takes up its position to await its train in the same manner as the other two Pacific's did. Note that all three 'Brits' had their tenders piled high with coal.

The final picture features 'Britannia' No.70013 making its way to Bressingham, through Garsdale after doing its bit on the famous 15 guinea special, the so called "last of the last". Seeing the immaculate engine effortlessly cantering along with the sun reflecting off its sides did not help the magnitude of that August day in 1968 to sink in. Alas, it was all over and it took some getting used to. I fell back into industrial steam and prolonged the agony somewhat because they too were not going to last for ever.